HELLO, HOW MAY I HELP YOU?

Sallie Parks

How may I Help You?

The title of this book originates from the voicemail greeting on my cell phone. Oftentimes, callers start engaging in conversation and then realize that they are not actually talking to me. This voicemail greeting is confusing for some callers. They feel that it is more fitting for a business, not a personal greeting. Callers fail to realize that sharing the Word of God is always a business, a principal activity in our lives. The quest to find ways to help others opens one's eyes to focus on answers about personal safety, admiration, learning, intentionality, and excellence for believers. This book will help believers navigate through various situations in life. It extends the purpose for life, as far as, being an obedient and helpful servant of God. Why not have a greeting that exudes assistance and servitude?

The intent of this book reminds us to seek God daily and to keep a line of communication open to Him. It is an assurance that demonstrates the faith of calling out to God, knowing that we will receive an answer to our prayers. The answer will not always be yes, only if your request aligns with His will. We can know for certain that God will sustain us until He provides an answer. If you are in pursuit of finding answers to life's questions, read this book to enhance your perspective in that area. It will also challenge your thinking while on mission for God. This book will help the readers to be more aware of their reasons for existence, which is to fulfill God's original plan. This should include worshiping God and serving others. It is a reminder that we should first seek the kingdom of God and His righteousness, and all other things will be added to our lives. (Matthew 6:33)

Our primary mission in life should be introducing people to Jesus and teaching them to follow Him. This is actually a part of our mission statement at church which references The Great Commission. Matthew 28: 18-20 states, "Then Jesus came to them and said, "All authority in heaven and on earth has been given to me. Therefore go and make disciples of all nations, baptizing them in the name of the Father and of the Son and of the Holy Spirit, and teaching them to obey everything I have commanded you. And surely I am with you always, to the very end of the age."

Why not share God's Word in our daily conversations with people? Remember, God's Word has the power to change lives, and He wants us to share His love and promises with everyone. In our conversations with others, God will work through us to accomplish His mission. Develop a relationship with God that includes praying daily and exemplifying His ways to the world in which we live.

Can you imagine calling out to God and suddenly realizing that it is His voicemail? Were you leaving a message rather than talking to Him? Wow, what a shock that is for anyone! This is not a possibility for believers. When we, as believers, call out to God, we never have to imagine talking to a tricky voicemail. Praying and seeking God daily strengthens our relationship with Him. God is always readily available to listen. He tells us in Psalm 145:18 that He is near to all who call on Him in truth.

The title of this book prompts me to share information that will be beneficial in daily life. **How may I help you?** My help is evident by directing individuals to God's Word to find answers to questions that we may not know or simply need further clarification. The content in this book will inspire us to seek God's wisdom for our personal knowledge and understanding. This will enhance our everyday endeavors. It guides people to participate in a deeper study of the scriptures. If you lack wisdom, God's Word provides the answers that you are seeking. James 1:5 says, "If any of you lack wisdom, you should ask God, who gives generously to all without finding fault, and it will be given to you."

Read, interpret, evaluate, and learn from the snippets that are presented in this book. Various questions are asked; scriptural references are provided; and words of encouragement are expressed as well. This is just the beginning; once believers read the scriptures that are provided in this text, they will soon realize that God has the answers to all questions imagined. Acquire knowledge to access the tools (cognition); get understanding to know the meaning (intention); gain wisdom to know how to apply (application). When we feel inquisitive, we can always rely on our Heavenly Father for the correct responses. This is an added blessing because God provides answers without finding fault with us. It eliminates doubt and any possibility of asking ourselves whether or not it is a dumb question. Remember He is our Creator and He has unique responses for all of us. God's Word is intentional because He knows the plans for us. Jeremiah 29:11 states, "For I know the plans I have for you, declares the Lord, plans to prosper you and not to harm you, plans to give you hope and a future." Through the Holy Spirit, we are equipped to receive answers with our spiritual eyes and ears.

Continue to study God's Word because your answers to life's questions are waiting to be found. The Bible has the answer to anything you might ask. Join me in the quest of seeking God to answer the following questions. Through life's experiences and conversations, I have heard these questions mentioned numerous times. God will direct you to the answers that will fit your needs. This book contains responses from researching the Bible, reading various commentaries, listening to sermons, and sharing my own life experiences.

____

____

____

____

____

____

How may I Help You?

Why are people reluctant to help each other to succeed?

Is it ever too late to ask for forgiveness for your sins?

If you are feeling that the world is against you, who do you turn to for help?

Do children think about faith?

How important is prayer?

Does God tell us what to think about in life?

Ultimately, who do you work for?

Who should come first in our lives?

Are you ashamed of the gospel?

Why is it important to have the right mindset in the world in which we live?

How may I Help You?

Question: Why are people reluctant to help each other succeed?

REFLECT ON THE SCRIPTURE: EXODUS 17:12-13

But Moses' hands became heavy; so they took a stone and put it under him, and he sat on it. And Aaron and Hur supported his hands, one on one side, and the other on the other side; and his hands were steady until the going down of the sun. 13 So Joshua defeated Amalekites and his people with the edge of the sword. (NKJV)

In today's society, it doesn't seem like anyone wants to help anyone else succeed, but there are people who are still willing to help others become successful. Just the other day, my hairstylist, Tina, shared with her clients how she constantly networks to help others gain employment. Her environment exudes this helpfulness. Her clients, Pam, Rose, Dawn, Mesa,

Mel, Mitzi, and Vania spend their precious time helping others to succeed as well. God has always orchestrated situations to provide support for us to illustrate His Glory. According to scripture, Moses received earthly help so Joshua would be successful in defeating the Amalekites. They were relentless people against God's chosen people. This event would not have been a success without God's divine intervention. When people feel that they do not have a support system for success, they begin to get overwhelmed with a sense of being alone. Be encouraged because God will provide people who will be there to help in achieving any goal, completing any task, or simply getting you through a tough situation. Allowing the right people to bring success into being is presented in the story of Moses, Aaron, and Hur as they stood above the battlefield waiting on Joshua to defeat the Amalekites. Moses had a relationship with God where he would call out to Him, and God would provide instruction and direction to be successful. Try developing that relationship with God, so that He will provide answers for you as well. By holding Moses' arms up for victory, Aaron and Hur were instrumental in aiding the defeat of the Amalekites. Moses told Joshua to go and fight the Amalekites. Moses also told him that he would be on the top of the hill with the staff of God in his hands. That feeling of "someone has my back" certainly empowered Joshua even more.

Knowing how to listen and receive an answer from God will certainly make a difference. Stay in constant communication with God by praying and asking Him to allow the Holy Spirit to guide you in the study of His Word. The scripture talks about how you should perceive God's Word in Psalm 119:18 where it states, "Open my eyes that I may see wonderful things in your law." Moses knew that as long as he followed God's instructions, he would be victorious. Believers can be assured that God will provide a support system for them as well. It builds confidence when believers depend on and trust in God for successful results. Again, Aaron, Moses's brother, and Hur held Moses's arms up so that Joshua would be successful in battle. **Who's going to hold your arms up during a crisis in your life?** This could be any number of people; for example, spouses, pastors, fathers, mothers, children, friends, or even co-workers. The list continues. When believers ask God for supporters, they are confident that He provides a plethora of individuals who will suffice. Reflect on your treatment of people. Each day, individuals should make a conscious effort to treat each other with respect and dignity because people never know when they themselves will need uplifting. Not only were Moses's arms held up for victory, his friends brought a stone for him to sit on. As believers, people go through trials and tribulations daily; they need the support of others. God's provision is exemplified in His words when He promises to never leave or forsake us. As a result, be encouraged because God will supply His followers with someone to hold their arms up during their battles as well.

How may I Help You?

Question: Is it ever too late to ask for forgiveness for your sins?

REFLECT ON SCRIPTURE: 1 JOHN 1:9

If we confess our sins, he is faithful and just and will forgive us our sins and purify us from all unrighteousness.

As long as you are living, you still have the opportunity to repent and turn away from sin. 1 John 1:9 states, "If we confess our sins, He is faithful and just to forgive us our sins and to cleanse us from all unrighteousness." Yes, this does mean if you have done something that you perceive unforgivable, God will forgive you. "Sin is an immoral act considered to be a transgression against divine law." (Oxford's Language Dictionary). Jehovah God is willing to forgive us, but we must repent. In repenting, we must stop whatever it is that we are doing wrong in order to make it right.

One day a young man decides to take money from his grandmother's purse because he gets tired of the other teenagers teasing him about being broke. He knows it is wrong, but he continues to steal from her for months. It is his responsibility to go by his grandmother's house after school to check on her every day. Finally, the young man's grandmother catches him taking money from her purse. It startles the grandmother in more ways than one. She cannot believe it. She looks at him with tears in her eyes and asked, "What are you doing?" The boy says, "Granny, I can explain." Being a woman of faith for many years, the first thing his grandmother asks is, "Which commandment did you break?" He replies with little thought, "Thou shalt not steal." The young man knows that he has sinned, but in his confession to his grandmother, he is quite ambiguous. He thinks due to him being teased, his grandmother will excuse it. On the other hand, he knows he is wrong because his grandmother will do anything for him. Because his family instilled morals and values in him, he asks his grandmother for forgiveness and promises to never do it again. His grandmother revisits the scripture, Proverbs 22:6 stating "Train up a child in the way he should go, and he will not depart from it when he is old." Parents, guardians, teachers, and anyone who has influence over children, utilize this scripture when children are in your care. Prepare children with the necessary tools to use in life. Give them scenarios of life lessons so they will be able to survive and maneuver through life with God's Word in their hearts. The grandmother knows deep down inside that her grandson is remorseful for what he has done. The young man ends up getting a part-time job, and the bullying comes to a halt. He pays his grandmother back and somehow his parents never finds out about it. That's an example of what can happen when you have God's Word instilled in children. It is never too late to ask for forgiveness for sins, no matter how big or small, young or old.

How may I Help You?

Question: If you are feeling that the world is against you, who do you turn to for help?

REFLECT ON THE SCRIPTURE: ROMANS 8:31

What then shall we say to these things? If God *is* for us, who *can be* against us?

Turn to God for help when you feel that the world is against you. Remember He is Our Provider. He is our Jehovah Jireh. Our Heavenly Father will place people in our lives to aid in the provision of support. We have shifted from an Old Testament scripture to a New Testament scripture to answer this question. Previously, we alluded to Moses's situation in the defeat of the Amalekites. The same God that was victorious in the provision of success for His people in Old Testament scriptures is the same God that we serve today. Help is always provided for us when it seems that the world is against us. It is evident in Romans 8:31. The first part of the two questions-**What then shall we say to these things?** You are probably wondering what things. Earlier in the Book of Romans, Paul expressed how Christ is greater than anything we face; those are the things that are being referenced. The interpretation is that we should look to God and not at what is in front of us. The second part of the question asks, "**If God *is* for us, who *can be* against us?** The answer is obvious - No one. No one or anything is comparable to the One and Only true God. He has many references; for example, in the book of Isaiah (9:6-7), he is presented as Wonderful Counselor, Mighty God, Everlasting Father, and Prince of Peace just to mention a few. As the Wonderful Counselor: who can provide the wisdom that we need? As the Mighty God: who can beat the enemies of sin and death? As the Everlasting Father: who can be the maker, redeemer, and sustainer of all things? As the Prince of Peace: who can bring back the world to God? The correct answer is no one because if God is for us, no one can be against us. God's Word assures us of this. Remember God gave us dominion over the things of this world. We just have to hold on to His promise where he says, we can do all things through Him who strengthens us. (Philippians 4:13) If you are feeling that the world is against you, turn to God for help. It sounds easy to answer with the response, "Turn to God for help." Do you know Him? Do you believe in Him? The suggestions originated from reading, searching the internet, and holding various conversations. It affords the opportunity to share habits that we can incorporate into our lives when we are seeking help.

To ask for and receive help from God, first accept Him as your Lord and Savior; develop a daily routine of praying and meditating on His Word; maintain a relationship with God; show gratitude; seek Him on behalf of others; and connect with other believers. In addition, when we seek God's help, scripture reassures us that the promise of answered prayer is dependent upon the phrase in scripture that specifies, "according to His will." 1 John 5:14 states, "This is the confidence we have in approaching God: that if we ask anything according to his will, he hears us." We have to trust God because He knows what is best for us in life.

____

____

____

____

____

How may I Help You?

Question: Do children think about faith?

REFLECT ON THE SCRIPTURE: MARK 11:24

Therefore I say unto you, what things so ever ye desire, when ye pray, believe that ye receive them, and ye shall have them.

More than you know, children are always thinking about faith. In today's society, it is important that we teach our children the importance of having faith. We teach them to pray and ask God for the desires of their hearts. Contrary to what we think about children, they do not always want material things, especially in this case with Kaitlyn. She only wants her family to be involved in her school activities. As Kaitlyn and her family sit at the table eating dinner, Kaitlyn asks her parents if they would come to the school's oratorical contest. The unanimous response is "No." Her parents have to work. Kaitlyn thinks that this time certainly someone will show up for her. She has been practicing, and it is her goal to win. Kaitlyn's wish is to have a family that will spend more time with her. Not only does Kaitlyn wish for her family's support, but she also prays about someone showing up to the event. Oftentimes, Kaitlyn reads a scripture or two with her grandfather. From those readings, she remembers a scripture that talks about God giving you the desires of your heart. Kaitlyn reflects on those words from scripture and implements them nightly into her prayers.

She knows that her classmates' parents and family members will be there. She knows that all of her family works except her grandfather, but of course, he will not show up because he never attends school events. He simply did not seem interested in things outside of farm life. She feels that she is special to her grandfather, but she does not want to take him out of his comfort zone. He is an awesome grandfather who loves the farm, church, and his family. He is also well respected within the community. She wants the people from her school to recognize his greatness as well. He taught her a lot about life in general and what she knows about the church. Kaitlyn wants that support to extend into her school environment. She ponders, "Why can't I just ask him?" She has a close relationship with her grandfather because he has been one of her main caretakers.

It is the big day at Pine Hill Elementary School. Kaitlyn has been accustomed to speaking on various programs, so she was not nervous at all. She only lacks support from her family. Her teacher, Mrs. Ervin is raving about Kaitlyn's speech to other faculty members before the contest even starts. As the little girl began to speak, she looks up and her grandfather is in the audience. Kaitlyn is extremely happy. Because of her faith in God, she realizes God has made it possible for someone from her family to show up. She would never have thought that it would have been her grandfather. Kaitlyn's performance is stellar, to say the least. Yes, she won!!! Her grandfather is so proud of her. Kaitlyn does not care that he was dressed in his farm working attire (overalls). Kaitlyn ignores the giggles from her classmates and basks in her triumph of winning the oratorical contest. Her grandfather shares the news with the rest of the family and they realize the importance of being involved in the children's lives more. Continue to encourage children to have faith because it can make a difference in their perspectives of trusting God. We must keep the faith and be assured that God will provide especially for children. According to many representatives of Christ, we should share Hebrews 11:6 with our children. *"And without faith it is impossible to please him, for whoever would draw near to God must believe that he exists and that he rewards those who seek him."* This encourages our children to first have faith in God and develop a relationship with Him. Children think about faith because we teach them to think about faith. As a result, we should be mindful of how we handle various situations in life because children are observing how we utilize faith.

How may I Help You?

Question: How important is prayer?

REFLECT ON THE SCRIPTURE: PHILIPPIANS 4:6-7

Do not be anxious about anything, but in every situation, by prayer and petition, with thanksgiving, present your requests to God. And the peace of God, which transcends all understanding, will guard your hearts and your minds in Christ Jesus.

It goes without thinking, prayer is essential for our lives. Prayer is extremely important because it is direct communication with God through our Lord and Savior Jesus Christ.

Do not use prayer as a time to tell God what you want, or a time to tell Him what to do. Prayer is a time to enhance your relationship with God and allow Him to tell you what His will is for you. Having the assurance that God is in our lives plus the fact that we are provided for each day without worry, is enough to warrant prayer as essential. Scripture tells us that if He provides for the birds and other animals, He will certainly provide for us. Matthew 6:26 states, "Look at the birds of the air; they do not sow or reap or store away in barns, and yet your heavenly Father feeds them. Are you not much more valuable than they?" Prayer is also important because it provides us the opportunity to express reverence, give thanks, and confess our sins. We were created to worship God and to fulfill His purpose for creating us. Prayer is very instrumental in worshiping God both individually and collectively. Believers get the opportunity to acknowledge God in prayer. During this quiet time, their concerns are not dependent on whether or not we have a small or large crowd. Matthew 18:20 states, "For where two or three gather in my name, there am I with them."

We all have acronyms that sometimes help or encourage us in our prayer life. My friend Ken shared that his pastor encouraged his congregation to pray by using the acronym ACTS. Ken shared, "First people should (A) Adore God- **Adoration,** (C) Confess sins-**Confession,** (T) Give thanks-**Thanksgiving,** (S) Supplicate-making our requests known-**Supplication.**" In life, there are times when we need direction in the enhancement of communicating with God. It makes a difference because for some individuals it gives direction, and it further ignites thinking about communicating with God. In addition to that acronym, various members from our Sunday school class especially Elizabeth, shared the acronym **PRAY** as well, which stands for **Praise, Repent, Ask, and Yield**. They mentioned that this was just free, flowing information, which I had never thought about. Whichever one you choose to use, should jump-start your prayers to be more intentional and meaningful. God always provides examples of things that are essential for daily living. In the books of Matthew and Luke, Jesus provides an example for us (model prayers). Luke 11:1 says, "One day Jesus was praying in a certain place. When he finished, one of his disciples said to him, "Lord, teach us to pray, just as John taught his disciples." Believers are fortunate to have those references to encourage them for direction and instruction in promoting prayer.

The need for prayer should be addressed because believers need to be reminded that prayer is essential communication with God. It reminds us of our purpose as believers; it fortifies our commitment to Him as well. In the reflection scripture for this question, an overall breakdown is given to us. First, "do not be anxious about anything, but pray about everything." So when believers pray, they must pray with thanksgiving in their hearts, and then ask God for His will to be done in their lives.

Prayer is very important in our lives for maintaining a relationship with God.

1 Thessalonians 5:16-18 reads, "Rejoice always, pray without ceasing, in everything give thanks; for this is the will of God in Christ Jesus for you". According to Chistianty.com, "to pray without ceasing" is to live with God in our hearts and minds, giving thanks for all things and relying on Him for strength. Remember when we pray without ceasing, we put everything into God's hands. John 15:7 further supports our need for prayer. It is profitable and beneficial to have that connectivity with our Lord and Savior. It says, "If you remain in me and my words remain in you, ask whatever you wish, and it will be done for you." What assurance we have in the power of prayer. How wonderful it is to be able to have this freedom to express ourselves to our Creator. God exemplifies order in Romans 12:2. It states, "Do not be conformed to this world, but be transformed by the renewal of our mind, that by testing you may discern what is the will of God, what is good and acceptable

and perfect." How important is prayer? Scripture demonstrates the importance of prayer. Ultimately, it is that open line of communication that Jesus made possible, "In Jesus's Name, we pray," the phase that concludes our prayers.

How may I Help You?

Question: Does God tell us what to think about in life?

REFLECT ON THE SCRIPTURE: PHILIPPIANS 4:8

Finally, brothers and sisters, whatever is true, whatever is noble, whatever is right, whatever is pure, whatever is lovely, whatever is admirable—if anything is excellent or praiseworthy—think about such things.

If people have been seeking the answer to this question, they can find it in the **BIBLE.** The answer is an astounding yes. God does reveal to us in His Word the things we should think about daily. First of all, the acronym B.I.B.L.E. is said to stand for, "Basic Instructions Before Leaving Earth. It certainly has the answers to all of life's questions. I became acquainted with this acronym years ago in a Wednesday night Bible study class, and it opened my eyes to what had been staring me in the face all along. It was probably common to everyone else, just not a big deal to some. For me, it was taken personally to follow those instructions in the Bible to live an abundant life here on earth. It was like finding *the "how to"* book of life. We discussed the acronym even in my Sunday School class and the pastor had a sermon on it as well. Of course, Pastor Daniel's explanation of the acronym was a lot more thorough. He stressed that the Bible provides so much more. Generally, we rely on the acronym as an "attention grabber" for the basics of daily living. It is imperative that we read and study the Word of God because it has the answers to all of life's questions. God tells us to think about those things that lead to an abundant life. Proceed to the book of Philippians in the New Testament. Paul points out in his final exhortations in Philippians 4:8, "Finally, brothers and sisters, whatever is true, whatever is noble, whatever is right, whatever is pure, whatever is lovely, whatever is admirable—if anything is excellent or praiseworthy—think about such things." All of these are positive attributes. As believers, we should think positively without fear of being ridiculed by others or allow others to cause anxiety due to how we think.

This takes us back to our prayer life. In the book of Philippians, Paul warns us not to be anxious or worried, but to pray about everything with thanksgiving. With this prayerful heart, rejoicing in the Lord, we are encouraged to think about those things that are excellent and praiseworthy. This was the topic of conversation when I saw my friends, Pastor and Mrs. Slater, in the shoe store one afternoon. We laughed about the way we were able to memorize the attributes of "how to think" found in the book of Philippians. I shared with them that I used "TAN RP L," which equates to a color (Tan) and my husband's initials (RP) plus the word (lovely). **(True, Admirable, Noble, Right, Pure, Lovely)** Certainly, this is simplicity at its best for some readers, but it works for the usage of mnemonic devices, which is a way of remembering. Yes, they are still being used today, especially in elementary schools. In turn, the Slaters used "**J Place**" as their mnemonic device. Whatever choice helps to retain the answer to the question will suffice. Just make a point to think about these attributes daily. Focus on-Truth, Nobility, Righteousness, Purity, Loveliness, and Admiration. The reality is we rarely hear these words, but they carry an aspiring connotation to the world.

In addition to Philippians 4:8, Romans 12:2 alludes to how we should think as well. It states, "Do not conform to the pattern of this world, but be transformed by the renewing of your mind.

Then you will be able to test and approve what God's will is—his good, pleasing and perfect will." As believers, we have to change our way of thinking. We cannot afford to think as the world thinks. We have to focus on the things that God has for us. Scripture also tells us to ask God to create a clean heart and renew a right spirit in us (Psalm 51:10). God sent Jesus to save us from our sinful way of thinking and to restore us to the perfect way that Jesus demonstrated. Again, continue to pray and study God's Word daily.

How may I Help You?

Question: Ultimately, who do you work for?

REFLECT ON THE SCRIPTURE:

Colossians 3:23-24 Whatever you do, work at it with all your heart, as working for the Lord, not for human masters, 24 since you know that you will receive an inheritance from the Lord as a reward. It is the Lord Christ you are serving.

To the general public, a Christian's response would be considered too loaded to say the least. Imagine saying that you work for the Lord. People in general would probably give you a side eye or a mere mumble. The mumble being revealed, "One of those again." It is optimistic to know that other believers share in the proclamation, "I work for The Lord." We work for the Lord because that is what we were created to do. Oftentimes, when people listen to sermons or inspirational programs, it ignites their thinking, especially when it pertains to enhancing work ethic and environments. People are inspired when they hear encouraging words to get them through another work day. God has always shown the perfect work pattern for us since the beginning. He worked six days and rested on the seventh day. One day, a speaker alluded to creation in a way that I never imagined. He said that God created **creation**, the stars, moon, water, land, etc; He created **creatures,** animals, fish, etc; and He created **creators,** humans. He went on to say that we were created to be creators because we are made in God's image. Just like our Father, we are committed to work and creativity. This is the mindset that we should adhere to in our daily lives. Believers should allow God to direct their paths in the assignments that He has provided for us. Working is a time to showcase the gifts and talents that God instilled in us. We should also be appreciative of the jobs that are assigned to us. John 5:17 says, "In his defense Jesus said to them, "My Father is always at his work to this very day, and I too am working."" This is where Jesus illustrates His refusal to stop performing miracles on the Sabbath. The religious leaders failed to recognize Jesus as the Messiah. They could not understand that Jesus was saying that His Father works every moment on behalf of creation, and so does He. God continually works on our behalf; therefore, we should work diligently on any task that is set before us.

There are situations where some people do not like their jobs for various reasons, so we must keep in mind that we are not working for humans, but for the Lord. With that sentiment, we are driven to work with all of our hearts. When we do anything for the Lord, our whole mindset will change. It requires honor and respect first and foremost. With that being said, no matter how insensitive your workplace boss is, you must exhibit respect. Show gratitude and be thankful to God for His provision. The Bible clearly states this in Colossians 3:23. It says, "Whatever you do, work at it with all your heart, as working for the Lord, not for human masters." Many of you have an automatic response to this. One would probably respond by saying something like "It is just a job, and they are not the boss of me." Is that truly the attitude that you want to display? Believers can be assured that we work for the Lord. Scripture supports the answer. It specifies in Colossians 3 that our desire to work should be driven by God in whatever we do. This scripture also encourages us to work with all of our hearts because we are working for the Lord, not for man. Believers know that we will receive our reward from the Lord. Having this affirmation or certainty about any job will promote successful results. This scripture encompasses everything you need to get through the day in any workplace. Verse 24 of Colossians chapter 3 further clarifies by stating, "Since you know that you will receive an inheritance from the Lord as a reward. It is the Lord that you are serving." We reap our benefits from God, not man. Again, be appreciative of the job you have been given because it is a blessing from God; he will sustain you through any situation you may encounter.

Ephesians 6:7 further defines the work ethic that we should uphold while on the job. It states, "Serve wholeheartedly, as if you were serving the Lord, not people." We find that hard sometimes when we are under the management of disgruntled or overbearing bosses. They tend to be disrespectful in their actions, tone, and speech. It is extremely difficult to deal with this type of behavior, but believers are encouraged to pray about it and allow God to handle it for them. Many can attest to certain situations where God will possibly move that boss away from the setting or move an employee to a job that is more desirable. Be obedient and work hard for the Lord because God can change any situation. In most cases, when one door closes, another opens in your favor.

How may I Help You?

Question: Who should come first in our lives?

REFLECT ON THE SCRIPTURE:

Exodus 20:3-Thou shalt have no other gods before me.

In response to the question of who should come first in our lives, many people would say family first, but that is not what biblical teaching suggests. God comes first in our lives. "Family comes first" is not an entirely erroneous answer because it is prioritized as well, maybe a strong second. Old Testament scriptures speak volumes about putting God first. God should be prioritized above any and all things. In the Ten Commandments, the very first commandant says, "Thou shalt have no other gods before me." Not only do Old Testament scriptures teach us about putting God first, but New Testament scriptures as well. Matthew 22:37-38 also alludes to putting God first. It says, "Jesus replied, Love the Lord your God with all your heart and with all your soul and with all your mind." 38 This is the first and greatest commandment. The essence of this scripture stresses that we should love Him with our emotions, desires, thought processes, and actions that we exert every day. Therefore, if we put God first, everything else will fall in the right place. One day, Amber and Jamie discussed a weekend getaway to the mountains in Gatlinburg, Tennessee. Jamie assured Amber that she would be available to travel any weekend during the Fall semester; therefore, Amber made all of the travel arrangements. Both girls were filled with excitement as they awaited this fun-filled event. Later, when Amber mentioned the date, Jamie shouted, "OMG! I can't go that weekend." Amber was not pleased about this because she had prepaid for the room reservations already; it was nonrefundable. The cousins had never been at odds about anything. They were as close as sisters. Jamie explained to Amber that she had to attend a conference with her theology class in another city. Apologetically, Jamie tried to explain the essence of this trip to Amber. This conference would be beneficial for Jamie's self-enhancement and her overall grade for that semester. Amber was heart-broken, but she realized how important this class was to Jamie. She also realized that this class was the reason that Jamie had made positive changes in her life. She knew that Jamie was adamant about her walk with God and she wanted to be an encouragement to Jamie as it related to prioritizing God. Even in a typical situation like this one, we should choose God first and anything related to His will being done in our lives. Amber chose not to put pressure on Jamie by trying to persuade her to change her plans. She simply asked one of her friends to go on the trip with her. As a result, they both enjoyed their trips, and their close bond was not affected. The answer to the question, "Who should come first?" is simple. God should always come first in any decision that we make. Proverbs 3:6 says," In all your ways acknowledge Him, And He shall direct your paths." That gives us the direction in which we should start our day. First, we should acknowledge God by praying and seeking Him for all decision-making. Amber realized that anything that is related to God should always come first whether big or small.

____

____

____

____

____

How may I Help You?

Question: Are you ashamed of the gospel?

REFLECT ON THE SCRIPTURE:

Luke 9:26 Whoever is ashamed of me and my words, the Son of Man will be ashamed of them when He comes in his glory and in the glory of the Father and of the holy angels.

To answer the question, "No, we are not ashamed of the Gospel; it gives us reassurance to say that we serve a living God." Being able to share the Gospel with others is illuminating to this world. It provides hope to a world that seems hopeless. What is the gospel? According to the article entitled "Gospel" (www.desiringgod.org), "the gospel is the good news that Jesus Christ, the Son of God, died for our sins and rose again, eternally triumphant over his enemies, so that there is now no condemnation for those who believe, but only everlasting joy."

It is difficult to believe that anyone could be ashamed of the gift of salvation, the good news of the coming of our Messiah. Being passionate about sharing the Good News motivates us to promote sharing His Word with people everywhere. We cannot afford to allow negative thinking to bring our momentum down. In addition, the site, (salvationcall.com) further explains that being ashamed of Jesus means being unwilling to identify yourself as a follower of Jesus. This happens because of fear, embarrassment, humiliation, ridicule, or disapproval." Any of these points can create a blockage to sharing the Gospel. Three of the four Gospels allude to being ashamed of the gospel. Jesus told His disciples not to be ashamed of Him or His words in Luke 9:26, Mark 8:38, and Matthew 10:32-33. The Book of Mark says, "For whoever is ashamed of Me and My words in this adulterous and sinful generation, of him the Son of Man also will be ashamed when He comes in the glory of His Father with the holy angels." Mark's gospel specifies even deeper with the prepositional phrase, "in this adulterous and sinful generation." We are reminded to stand firm while we are still on earth and to remain faithful.

Were people ashamed of the Gospel during COVID-19? The occurrence of the pandemic presented an opportunity to represent their faith in God. It was one of those times when people were happy to be associated with the Gospel. They understood that whatever happened, Jesus had already paid it all. During the time of COVID-19, it seemed that many focused their attention on Psalm 91. This particular Book in Psalms centers on God's protection. People felt that they could only turn to and depend on God. What a wonderful sentiment we recognize when we become totally dependent on Jesus. The Psalm focuses on God's provision when dealing with pestilence (disease), war, terror, enemies, and darkness. It was displayed on personal messages, YouTube, TikTok, emails, and an array of media platforms. Overall, Psalm 91 gave people a sense of calm and assurance that God would protect them from the pandemic. Like never before, people were calling on the **Name of Jesus**, believers, and non-believers. It reminded me of the scripture, Romans 10:13, which states, "For everyone who calls on the name of the Lord will be saved." Hopefully, people are keeping up the momentum in their trust and dependence on the Lord. How wonderful it is to be aware of the Gospel! That was a time to embrace and share the gospel even more. This is a reminder to constantly keep the name of Jesus in our hearts and minds every day, not just in troubled times. Also, according to Philippians 2:11, "and every tongue acknowledges that Jesus

Christ is Lord, to the glory of God the Father." Paul wanted everyone to know the importance of having the same mindset as Christ. We learn through it all that God gets the glory when we acknowledge the Lordship of Jesus. Many called on Jesus during this unrecognized time, but as a result, God received the glory because He was victorious once again in the outcome of the pandemic. People wanted to connect to the Word of God like never before. In addition, Psalm 91:2 says, "I will say of the LORD, He is my refuge and my fortress, my God, in whom I trust." This verse supports who God is to us and our overall need for Him daily. He is our "go-to" for all things, our protection in times of trouble, and our confidant to keep our secrets. In researching, I found many scripture references answering the question of whether or not we should be ashamed of the gospel. Romans 1: 16 states, "For I am not ashamed of the gospel, for it is the power of God for salvation to everyone who believes, . . . " Paul discusses this in his letter as he covers the topic of the righteous living by faith. As a result, we should exemplify our love for the gospel, not only in our words but our actions. If we are truly living by faith, we are never ashamed of the gospel.

How may I Help You?

Question: Why is it important to have the right mindset in the world in which we live?

REFLECT ON THE SCRIPTURE:

Romans 12:22 Do not conform to the pattern of this world, but be transformed by the renewing of your mind. Then you will be able to test and approve what God's will is—his good, pleasing and perfect will.

Every day people are being teased or ridiculed for not being like everyone else. It is important to know that scripture encourages us not to be like the world in which we live because we are made in God's image. The world does not always display things that represent God's image. He has given this earth to us as a temporary home. How are we spending this time? Scripture points to the book of Hebrews to remind us that while we are waiting for our permanent home, we should live in preparation for God's promised place for us. We should live with a kingdom mindset. Hebrews 13:14 states, "For this world is not our home; we are looking forward to our everlasting home in heaven." While we are here on earth, we should put others first, help the needy, care for the sick, and share the love of Christ. These are just a few ways we can spend our time as we wait to move to our permanent residence. We are also reminded in Matthew 6:19 which says, "We should not fall in what the world values. Do not lay up for yourselves treasures on earth, where moth and rust destroy and where thieves break in and steal." Not being ungrateful, but we should want better than the things that this world offers. Believers must possess the right mindset. We can find these better things in Christ Jesus by serving others. Romans 12:2 is one of several verses that teaches us not to live as the world suggests, but to change our thoughts to the way God wants us to think and to live out His will for us. Our reflection scripture again says, "Do not be conformed to this world, but be transformed by the renewal of your mind, that by testing you may discern what is the will of God, what is good and acceptable and perfect."

Every day after school, Ms. Henderson would sit in her car and read the bible before she would go home. She started isolating herself three to four months before being labeled anti-social by her coworkers. She thought they were her friends. Ms. Henderson was known as the social butterfly of the workplace. Daily, she would hang around after work to ensure that everyone had a great day and encouraged the employees to look forward to the upcoming day. She was loved by everyone. One day I noticed her sitting in her car weeping, and I asked her if everything was okay and she responded yes. Although her words were positive, she possessed a different demeanor. Ms. Henderson began talking about her mother, who was in the nursing home. She shared how deeply concerned she felt about her health. She confessed that she was aware that some of the coworkers thought it was odd for her to sit in her car alone, but she did not care about their opinions at this point. Ms. Henderson confessed, "All I try to do is bring joy to everyone, and this is what I get. A time when I need my coworkers the most, they are unavailable." After venting about her frustrations, Ms. Henderson seemed to have gotten comfort from the conversation. She had the opportunity to express her feelings about dealing with her mom's healing process and the employees' reactions. We never know what others are going through. In this case, rather than jumping on the bandwagon and thinking negatively about Mrs. Henderson, the co-workers should have supported her by at least inquiring about the drastic change in her behavior. Being connected by similar faith, some of the coworkers prayed for her mother's recovery and asked Ms. Henderson for forgiveness. People in general can easily take sides when the world thinks it is weird, but keep the teachings of Christ in mind. It will make a difference in how to handle all situations. Ephesians 4:23 also tells us to "be renewed in the spirit of your mind." When you are renewing your mind, you should consider identifying negative thoughts or lies and replace them with truth. Study God's Word daily and be prepared to embrace God's truth. Surely there have been times in life when people have talked negatively about various issues, but do not change your thinking to line up with the world's. Remember, we cannot think like the people of this world because with a renewed mind, we can receive God's perfect will for us. As a result, follow God's suggestion in 2 Corinthians 10:5: "We demolish arguments and every pretension that sets itself up against the knowledge of God, and we take captive every thought to make it obedient to Christ." Because we are in a spiritual battle for our minds, we must renew our minds with the Word of God, not allowing the enemy to gain control over what we think. It is imperative that we maintain the right mindset in the world in which we live.

About the Author

Sallie Stabler Parks, a native of Wilcox County, now calls Montgomery, Alabama home. A retired teacher, she's earned multiple Teacher of the Year Awards during her career. Even in retirement, she's passionate about literacy education, teaching Sunday School and Life Group classes. Alongside her writing endeavors of children's books and devotionals, she cherishes moments spent with her family and friends. Married with two adult children, she continues to impact lives through her dedication to teaching and writing.